Puzzling Through Mark

Puzzling Through Mark

Carine Mackenzie

CHRISTIAN FOCUS PUBLICATIONS

© 1993 Christian Focus Publications
ISBN 1 85792 056 2

Published by
Christian Focus Publications
Geanies House, Fearn, Tain, Ross-shire
IV20 1TW, Scotland, Great Britain

Cover design by Donna Macleod
Cover illustration by Alan Baker

Printed and bound in Great Britain by
Cox & Wyman Ltd, Reading, Berks

Contents

Introduction

Mark wrote the book called the Gospel of Mark. What does Gospel mean?

Score out the letters M A R and K and see what is left.

M	R	M	K	A	K	M	A	M
R	G	O	O	D	R	A	R	A
M	K	R	M	R	A	R	A	K
K	A	K	N	E	W	S	K	R
A	K	R	M	K	M	A	M	R

Three other men wrote a Gospel. They are Matthew, Luke and John. They all tell us the good news about the Lord Jesus coming to the world to save sinners.

> **God** so loved the world that he gave his one and **only son** that whoever believes in him shall not **perish** but have **eternal life**. (John 3.16.)

Write down the first letter of the words in bold from the verse above.

Gospel

John the Baptist (1.1-8)

John the Baptist was a preacher. He travelled around the desert area of Judea preaching to the people who came out from the towns to hear him. 'You must repent and turn from your sins and ask God to forgive you,' he said.

John lived very simply.
What did he wear? Solve the code to find out.

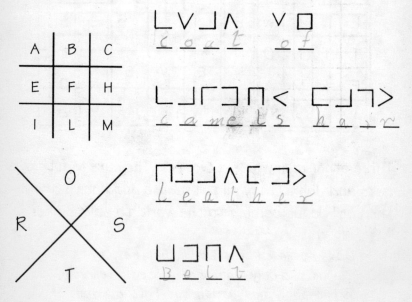

coat   of

camels hair

Leather

Belt

His diet was very strange too. The following vowels are missing from the words. Fit them in.

E I O O U

L O C U S T S
W I L D H O N E Y

8

John the Baptist's main message was to point people to the Lord Jesus Christ. Jesus was much more important than John.

W	I	L	L	C	O	M	E	O	N	E
E	H	O	N	G	O	F	W	H	O	M
M	T	W	O	R	T	H	Y	T	S	O
R	E	T	N	A	N	D	U	O	E	R
E	H	O	W	E	I	T	N	S	S	E
T	T	N	O	D	P	O	O	T	A	P
F	I	M	A	I	S	L	A	D	N	O
A	N	A	H	T	L	U	F	R	E	W

START HERE

Work round the grid into the centre to find what John said about Jesus.

After me will come one more
powerful than I, the thong of
whose sandals I am not worthy to
stoop down and undo (Mark 1.7.)

Baptism (1.9-13)

Jesus was baptised in the River Jordan by John. When he came out of the water, the heavens were opened and the Holy Spirit appeared to him in the form of a dove. God the Father spoke to Jesus from heaven.

What did he say?

Start at the arrow and work round the circle using every third letter.

DOIY MAOIMULWAOERVLEELMWPYILSTEOHANYSWOEHU

You are my son whom I love

with you I am well pleased

(Mark 1.11)

First Disciples (1. 14-20)

Jesus went to Galilee and preached the good news or Gospel of God. He told the people that the time had come when it was important that they do something.

What should they do?
Start at the centre of the spiral and find what Jesus told the people to do, and what he tells us to do.

repent and believe the good news (Mark 1.15)

When Jesus was walking along the shore of the Sea of Galilee, he saw two men fishing with a net in the lake.

Moving from left to right along each line pick out every third letter to find what Jesus said to the two men.

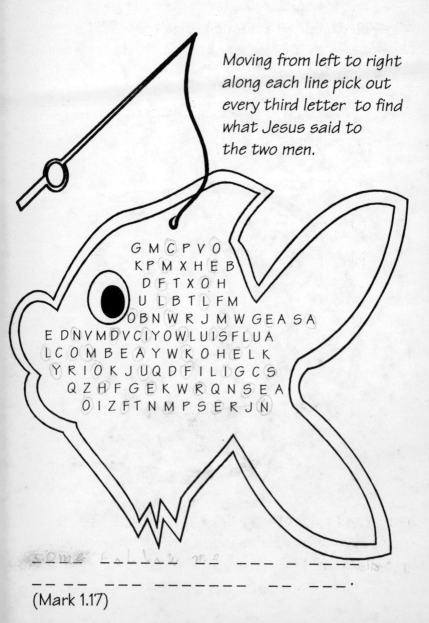

```
    G M C P V O
    K P M X H E B
     D F T X O H
     U L B T L F M
    O B N W R J M W G E A S A
E D N V M D V C I Y O W L U I S F L U A
L C O M B E A Y W K O H E L K
Y R I O K J U Q D F I L I G C S
  Q Z H F G E K W R Q N S E A
   O I Z F T N M P S E R J N
```

_come _ _ _ _ _ _ _ us ___ _ ____
__ __ ___ _____ __ ___.

(Mark 1.17)

These men were Simon and his brother Andrew. What did they do when Jesus spoke to them?

Starting at A read down and up the columns following the arrows.

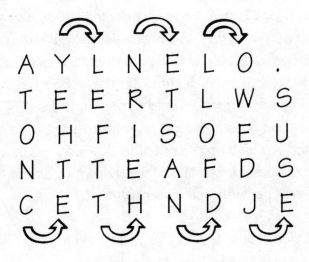

__ ____ ____ ____ _____

____ ___ _____ _____ .

(Mark 1. 18)

James and his brother John also left their fishing business and followed Jesus. They became Jesus' first disciples.

Jesus Heals a Paralysed Man
(2.1-12)

Jesus had power to heal those who were ill in body and mind. He helped people with all sorts of diseases and disabilities. Jesus was preaching in a house in Capernaum one day. So many people gathered that the house was full and there was even a crowd outside the door. Four men decided to take their paralysed friend to see if Jesus would cure him. There was such a crowd they could not get anywhere near Jesus. They decided to climb up the outside stairway, make a hole in the roof and lower their friend down to Jesus. Their faith and persistence was rewarded.

What did Jesus say to the paralysed man? Unscramble the letters to find out.

ONS UOYR
NSIS REA
GIVNORFE

Some proud men objected to his words. But Jesus showed his power by healing the man.

What did he say?
Can you crack the coded message.

G△O   UP   ◯AK△

Y◖U R   MA◯   AND

G◖   H◖M△   E = △
                O = ◖
                T = ◯

Everyone was amazed and praised God. 'We have never seen anything like this,' they said.

Twelve Apostles
(3.13-19)

Jesus chose twelve men to be special helpers for him.
They were called apostles or disciples.
Find all the disciples' names in the grid. Note that the
name James appears twice.

SIMON PETER	PHILIP	JAMES
ANDREW	BARTHOLOMEW	THADDAEUS
JAMES	MATTHEW	SIMON
JOHN	THOMAS	JUDAS ISCARIOT

J	J	O	H	N	J	E	A	S	P	U	S	S
S	U	S	A	I	D	G	N	O	H	I	N	I
T	O	D	I	A	L	L	D	T	I	H	E	M
W	W	O	A	M	R	L	R	D	L	A	N	O
E	D	P	R	S	O	E	E	A	I	C	H	N
H	T	H	T	E	I	N	W	G	P	O	O	P
T	D	N	H	E	S	S	S	E	M	A	J	E
T	W	S	O	T	E	O	C	A	L	L	C	T
A	R	E	M	A	M	T	I	A	O	N	T	E
M	H	E	A	N	A	T	H	E	R	D	I	R
S	C	I	S	P	J	L	E	S	W	I	E	N
T	H	A	D	D	A	E	U	S	T	O	O	U
T	W	E	M	O	L	O	H	T	R	A	B	T

The remaining letters in the wordsearch spell out what Jesus wanted and still wants his followers to do; and how they obeyed him.

_ _ _ _ _   _ _ _ _   _ _   _ _ _ _   _ _ _

_ _ _   _ _ _ _ _   _ _ _   _ _ _ _ _ _   _ _ _

_ _ _ _   _ _ _ _   _ _   _ _ _   _ _ _ _ _ _ _ _.

_ _ _ _   _ _ _   _ _ _ _ _ _ _ _   _ _ _ _

_ _ _.

Jesus sent the twelve chosen disciples to the villages in twos. They took no extra clothes with them, no money, no bag.

Colour in the letters without a dot to find the important instruction in their message.

17

Parable of the Sower (4.1-20)

Jesus told a story to a crowd of people gathered on the lake shore. His platform was a fishing boat out on the water. He told the story about a farmer who sowed seed on his farm. The seed fell on four different types of ground.

Follow the lines to find what happened in each type of soil.

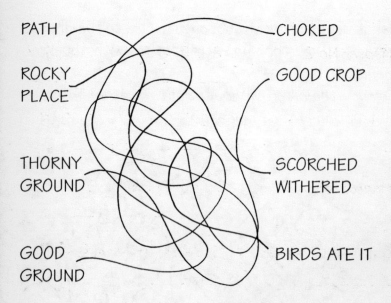

PATH

ROCKY PLACE

THORNY GROUND

GOOD GROUND

CHOKED

GOOD CROP

SCORCHED WITHERED

BIRDS ATE IT

Jesus told the story to teach his listeners. These special stories are called parables and they have an important meaning.

More Seeds (4.26-29)

Jesus told another story about the seed - teaching the good news of the Gospel. The farmer sows the seed and it grows. It produces a stalk, then an ear and then a fully grown plant. Whether the farmer watches the crop or sleeps in his bed, the seed still goes on growing. The gospel message is like the seed. It has power to change people's hearts and lives.

Put the letters from the second grid into the correct places.

(Hebrews 4.12)

1	2	3	4	5	6	7	8	9	10	11	12	13

3	12	9	4	1	13	6	10	2	7	11	5	8
E				T		O	O	H	R	F	W	D
D	N	I		G	G	S	V	O		I	I	L
D	I	V		A	T	C	E	N	T		A	I
D		H	G	J		S	E	U			E	T
O	D		U	T		H	A	H	T	N	G	S
T	F	S	I	A		U		T	D	O	T	E
E		T		T		E		H	A		H	R

22

Mustard Seed (4.30-34)

'The kingdom of heaven is like a very tiny mustard seed,' said Jesus. The very little seed grows into a large garden plant. The branches are so big that they can give shelter to the birds. The kingdom of God may have a very small beginning but it will flourish and prosper and its greatness and power will be seen by all the world.

Use the code to find out about the kingdom of God.

```
M U S T A R D   S E E D
1 2 3 4 5 6 7   3 8 8 7
```

4h8   king7o1   of   4h8   wo6L7
___   _____   __   ___   _____

h53 b8co18 4h8 king7o1 of o26
___ _____ ___ _____ __ ___

Lo67 an7 of hi3 Ch6i34, an7
____ ___ __ ___ _____ ___

h8 will   68ign fo6 8v86 an7
__ ____   _____ ___ ____ ___

8v86
____

(Rev.13.15)

Jesus calms the Storm (4.35-41)

After preaching and teaching at the lakeside, Jesus invited his disciples to go with him to the other side of the lake. So they set sail in the boat. Suddenly a fierce storm came up. The boat was nearly swamped with water.

Use the times on the clock to solve the code.

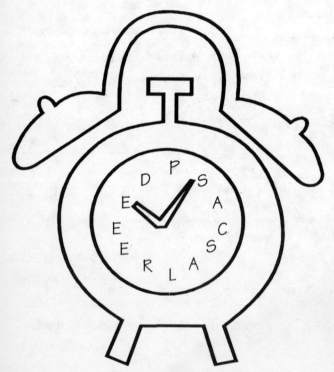

The disciples were 1.3.5.7.9.11.

_ _ _ _ _ _

Jesus was 2.4.6.8.10.12.

_ _ _ _ _ _

The disciples woke Jesus up. 'Don't you care if we drown?' they shouted. Jesus told the wind and the waves to be quiet and still. Immediately it was completely calm. Jesus was surprised that the disciples were so afraid. They seemed to have no...

1.3.5.7.9.

_____

Use the dials of the telephone to solve this code.

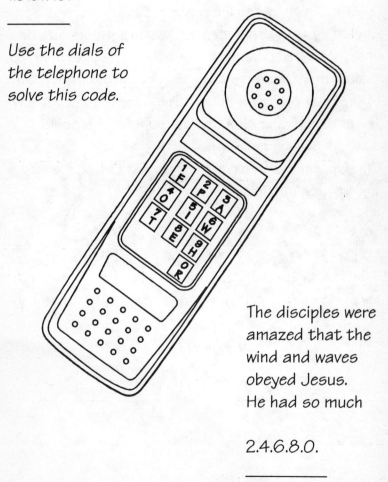

The disciples were amazed that the wind and waves obeyed Jesus. He had so much

2.4.6.8.0.

_____

Healing of a
Demon-possessed
Man(5.1-20)

When Jesus got out of the boat after crossing the lake, a man with an evil spirit met him. His name was Legion (which means many) because he was possessed by many demons. He lived in a graveyard, and was a danger to himself and others. People tried to chain him up because they were so afraid of him, but he broke the chains every time. When the man saw Jesus coming, he shouted as loudly as he could.

The sentence is written backwards. Put the words and letters in the correct order.

?DOG   HGIH   TSOM   EHT   FO

NOS   SUSEJ   EM   HTIW   TNAW

UOY   OD   TAHW

_ _ _ _   _ _   _ _ _   _ _ _ _   _ _ _ _   _ _

_ _ _ _ _   _ _ _   _ _   _ _ _   _ _ _ _

_ _ _ _   _ _ _?

Jesus ordered the evil spirit to come out of the man. A large herd of pigs was feeding on the hill-side close by. 'Let us go into those pigs,' begged the demons. Jesus gave them permission and they went into the animals. The 2000 pigs went berserk and they ran down the hill into the lake and drowned.

The pig herders saw what had happened and ran to tell the townspeople. Everyone came to see the spectacle. They saw that Legion had completely changed.

What was he like now? Move from square to square through the gaps - starting at S.

S	I	N	D
I	M	T	H
T	T	I	G
D	G	N	I
R	E	S	R
S	S	I	H
E	D	I	N

_ _ _ _ _ _ _

_ _ _ _ _ _ _   _ _   _ _ _

_ _ _ _ _   _ _ _ _

The man wanted to go away with Jesus but he had other work for him to do.

Follow the trail and discover what this was

_____

_____

_____

All the people were amazed.

Jairus' Daughter (5.21-24,35-43)

A large crowd of people gathered round Jesus when he was beside the lake. An important church ruler called Jairus came anxiously to Jesus and fell down at his feet. He told Jesus his problem.

What was it? Solve the code. A=1, B=2, C=3 etc

13.25.   12.9.20.20.12.5.   4.1.21.7.8.20.5.18.

_ _   _ _ _ _ _ _   _ _ _ _ _ _ _ _

9.19.   4.25.9.14.7.

_ _   _ _ _ _ _

'Please come and heal her' begged Jairus. Jesus was delayed and soon some messengers came from Jairus' house with bad news.
The little girl had died.
'Don't bother asking Jesus to come now,' they said.
Follow the lines to find out what Jesus said to Jairus.

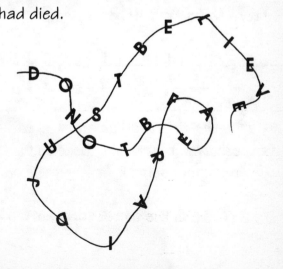

29

When Jesus reached the house he took five people into the room with him.

Who were they?

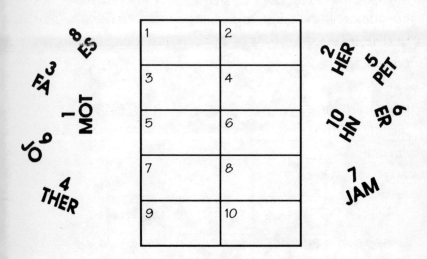

1	2
3	4
5	6
7	8
9	10

8 ES
3 FA
1 MOT
9 JO
4 THER

2 HER
5 PET
10 HN
6 ER
7 JAM

Jesus took the little girl's hand. Unscramble the letters to find out what he said.

ETTLLI   RIGL   TGE   PU

_ _ _ _ _ _   _ _ _ _   _ _ _   _ _

At once the girl stood up and walked. Jesus showed his great power by raising her to life. He showed his love and compassion by issuing the order.

VIEG   EHR   HISMOTEGN   OT   TAE

_ _ _ _   _ _ _   _ _ _ _ _ _ _ _ _   _ _   _ _ _

The Sick Woman(5.25-34)

On the way to Jairus' house Jesus met another needy person. A lady had been ill for twelve years with internal bleeding. She had tried lots of doctors, but no-one could help her. Her illness became worse. She had heard about Jesus and pushed through the crowd to reach him.

What did she say? Work round the grid in a clockwise direction into the centre starting at bottom left hand corner.

S	T	T	O	U	C
U	W	I	L	L	H
J	I	E	D	B	H
I	S	L	■	E	I
F	E	A	E	H	S
I	H	T	O	L	C

↑

__ _ ____ _____ ___

_____ _ ____ __ _____ .

Immediately the bleeding stopped and she felt better. No-one else saw what the woman had done, but Jesus knew that he had healed someone.

He turned round and asked a question.

Fill in the missing vowels.

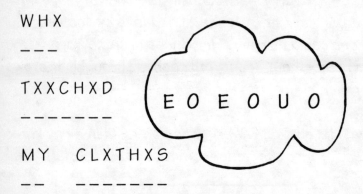

W H X

_ _ _

T X X C H X D

_ _ _ _ _ _ _

MY   C L X T H X S

_ _   _ _ _ _ _ _ _

E O E O U O

The disciples were amazed at him asking such a question in this pushing and shoving crowd of people. Jesus kept looking round. Then the woman came forward trembling, and told him the whole story. Jesus comforted her with the following words.

Put the jigsaw pieces in the correct place

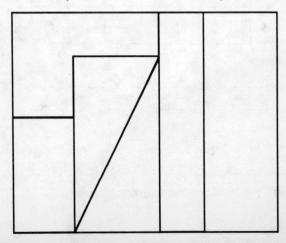

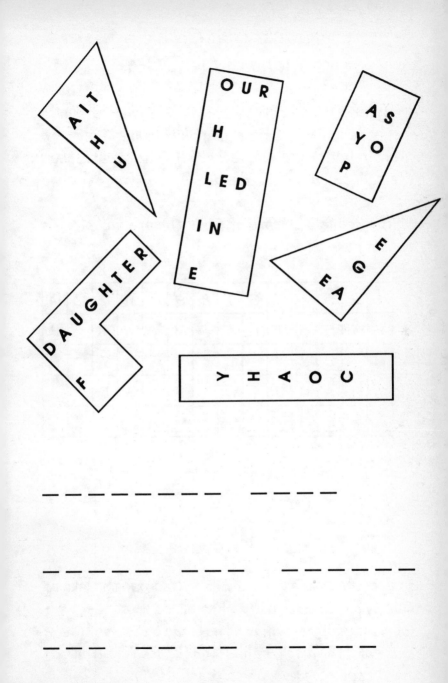

_ _ _ _ _ _   _ _ _ _

_ _ _ _   _ _   _ _ _ _ _

_ _ _   _ _   _ _   _ _ _ _

33

Jesus and his disciples were very busy speaking to people, teaching them, helping and healing. They were so busy that they did not even have time to eat. Jesus was concerned for his friends.

What was his suggestion? Fill in the missing spaces by using the letters below.

	1	2	3	4	5	6	7	8	9	10	11	12	13	14
a	H		S	A	I	D	C		M		W	I		H
b	M		B	Y	Y		U		S		L	V		S
c			A	Q	U	I			P	L	A	C		
d	A	N	D	G			S		M				S	

E at 2a, 10a, 2b, 10b, 13b, 7c, 13c, 5d, 10d, 12d.
O at 8a, 6b, 2c, 8d.
R at 8b, 11d.
T at 13a, 1c, 8c, 6d, 14d.

So they got into a boat and sailed across the lake to a lonely place. Lots of people realised what they were doing and walked round on the land to the spot where Jesus and the disciples had landed. Jesus had pity on these people and began to teach them.

As it came near to evening the disciples suggested that Jesus should send the crowd home. They would all be hungry by now.

'Give them something to eat yourselves,' answered Jesus.

'It would take a large sum of money to buy enough bread to feed this crowd,' they replied.

'How many loaves do you have?' he asked. 'Go and find out!'

How much food did the disciples discover?

Jesus told the people to sit down on the grass in groups of fifty and one hundred. There were 5000 men with women and children too. What a huge crowd!

What did Jesus do before he broke the food into pieces?

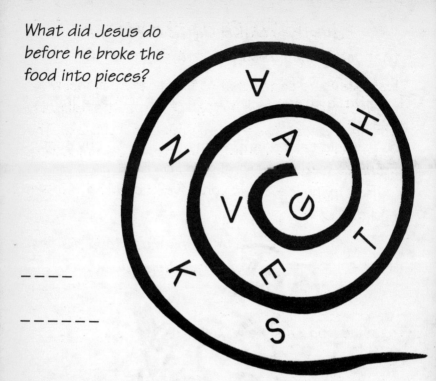

_ _ _ _

_ _ _ _ _ _

He handed the pieces to his disciples and they shared them out to the groups of people. Everyone had enough to eat. No-one was hungry any more. There was even some left over.

How many baskets were left over?

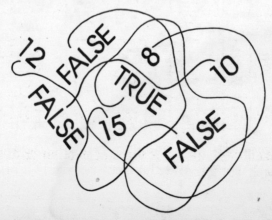

Jesus Walks on the Water
(6.45-56)

Jesus went up to the mountains to pray alone, while his disciples rowed the boat back across the lake. By evening, the boat was still in the middle of the lake. The wind was blowing against them and the disciples were struggling with the oars.

In the middle of the night Jesus went out to join the disciples in the boat. His power was shown as he performed another miracle. He walked on top of the water!

The disciples thought Jesus was a ghost, and were scared. Jesus' voice came out of the darkness to reassure and encourage them.

Follow the arrows and see what he said.

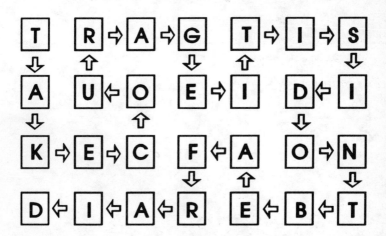

Then he climbed into the boat with them and the wind died down.

Faith of the Syro-Phoenician Woman (7.24-30)

A Greek lady from Syro-Phoenicia had a little daughter who was very sick. She was possessed by an evil spirit.

Jesus was visiting a place near the town of Tyre. The Greek lady heard he was there and went to ask him if he would help her daughter. This lady was not of the Jewish religion. Jesus said a very strange thing to her. 'Let the children eat all the food they want. It is not right to take the children's bread and throw it to their dogs.' By this he meant that he had come first of all for the Jewish people.

The woman's answer pleased Jesus so much that he rewarded her faith and healed her daughter there and then. What was her reply?

START HERE

EAT YES LORD BUT EVEN THE DOGS UNDER THE TABLE CRMBS THE CHILDREN'S

___ ____ ___ ____

___ ____ _____

___ _____

___ ___

_____

_____ ___

The woman went home to find her child completely better. Jesus' power and teaching and love is not just for the Jewish people, but for all other nations too. Anyone in the world can come to him.

Jesus Feeds the Four Thousand (8.1-13)

A large crowd of people gathered in a remote place to hear Jesus' teaching. They stayed with him for three days without anything to eat. Jesus felt sorry for them and did not want to send them home hungry.

'Where can we get enough bread to feed this crowd of people?' the disciples asked.

'How many loaves do you have?' replied Jesus.

'Seven!' was the answer.

What did Jesus do then?

Read the letters round the grid starting at the lower left hand corner.

V	E	T	H	A	N	K	S
A	T	T	O	H	I	S	B
G	I	I	V	E	T	D	R
S	E	G	O	W	O	I	O
U	V	O	R	D	T	S	K
S	A	T	C	E	H	C	E
E	G	S	E	L	P	I	T
J	D	A	E	R	B	E	H

JESUS GAVE THANKS, BROKE THE
BREAD, GAVE IT TO HIS DISCIPLES
TO GIVE TO THE CROWD.

He did the same with the few small fish that someone had brought with him. Everybody had enough to eat. What amazing power Jesus had. He fed 4000 men with a few loaves and fishes.

What did the disciples pick up afterwards? Shade in the second box and every alternate box to discover the answer which will stand out.

D	P	B	Q	S
O	C	G	E	F
L	A	R	B	E
C	E	E	T	N
E	N	O	E	V
G	S	F	F	D
F	M	K	Y	E
I	O	C	U	H
T	K	E	D	N
J	F	I	L	L
O	W	N	V	B
X	F	M	S	L
V	N	P	B	A
P	O	J	O	K
E	R	I	R	S
H	O	S	F	T
R	U	E	A	K

41

Peter's Confession of Christ (8.27-30)

As Jesus was walking one day with his disciples, he asked them 'Who do people say I am?' They told him what people were saying.
Unscramble the letters.

Some say you are H N J O H T E S A P B I T T

– – – –   – – –   – – – – – – – –

others say L A E J I H

– – – – – –

and others R E P P O T H

– – – – – – –

Then Jesus asked 'Who do you say I am?' Peter gave a firm answer.

– – –   – – –   – – –   –   – – – – –

O	T	C	R	I	E	Y	T	H	H	A	U	E	R	S
2	7	10	5	13	9	1	15	8	11	4	3	6	12	14

It meant that they truly believed that he was the Saviour, the one chosen by God to save his people from their sins.

The Transfiguration (9.2-12)

Jesus took Peter, James and John up to a high mountain. When they were quite alone, an amazing thing happened. Jesus' appearance changed. His clothes became dazzling white. Elijah and Moses came and talked with him. Then a cloud appeared around them. God's voice spoke from the cloud. When they looked again, they saw no one else except Jesus.

Find out what he said.
Note every third letter round the circle

____ __ __ ___

____ _ ____.

_____ __ ___.

Who is the Greatest?(9.33-37)

One day the disciples were arguing. 'Which one of us is the greatest?' 'Is it me?' 'No, it is me!' 'What are you arguing about?' Jesus asked them. They were too ashamed to say. But Jesus knew. He told the friends what it meant to be really great. It was not what they expected.

Work out the code.

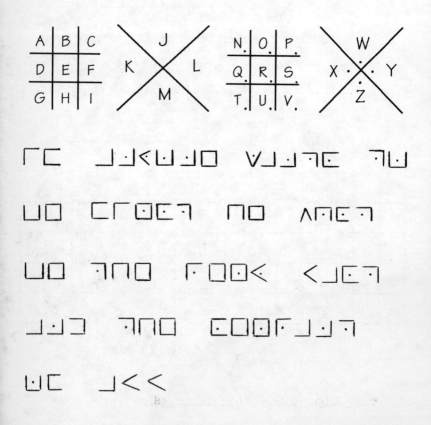

Jesus brought a little child to the company. He lifted him up in his arms and taught the disciples another valuable lesson.

Put the columns in the correct order.

1	2	3	4	5	6	7	8	9	10	11	12	13	14	15

6	2	12	5	8	14	1	15	10	7	13	3	11	9	4
U	F	O	O	W	E	I		L		M		C	E	Y
T		I	T	E	D	A		C	L	L	L	H		I
	N	Y	Y	A	U	I		E	N	O			M	M
M	E	A	O		D	W		E	E	N	L		M	C
H	O	T	W		M	G	E	E	O		D	N	S	

Jesus cares for children like you.

The Little Children and Jesus
(10.13-16)

Mothers and fathers brought their little children to Jesus so that he would touch them. The disciples were annoyed with them and tried to send the children away. Had they forgotten what Jesus had said about welcoming children? (see page 45).

Jesus was glad that the children were brought to him.

What did he say? Read the message backwards start- ing at the bottom line and working to the top of the page.

eseht
sa hcus ot
sgnoleb doG
fo modgnik
eht rof
meht rednih
ton od dna
em ot emoc
nerdlihc
elttil
eht teL

Jesus said that if anyone wanted to enter the kingdom of God he would have to become like what?

A = 8
C = 7
D = 6
E = 5
H = 4
I = 3
L = 2
T = 1

8   2 3 1 1 2 5
−   − − − − − −

7 4 3 2 6
− − − − −

What did Jesus do then? Put words in correct grids.

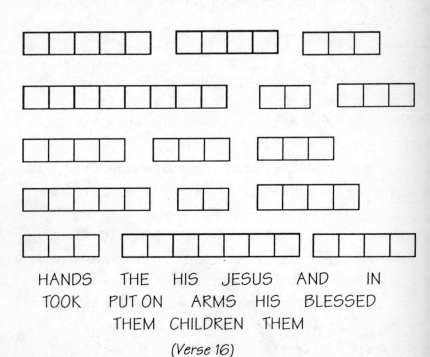

HANDS   THE   HIS   JESUS   AND   IN
TOOK   PUT ON   ARMS   HIS   BLESSED
THEM   CHILDREN   THEM

(Verse 16)

Rich Young Ruler (10.17-31)

A rich young man came to Jesus with a very important question.

W H _ T   M _ S T   _   D _   T _

_ N H _ R _ T   _ T _ R N _ L   L _ F _ ?

Insert the vowels in the spaces.

A A E E E E I I I I O O U

Jesus directed the young man to the Ten Commandments (These are found in Exodus chapter 20).

'I have kept all these commandments since I was a boy,' he declared. How little he understood!

Jesus could see that there was something that this man loved too much. It was keeping him from truly loving God.

'Go and sell all your possessions and give the money to the poor,' said Jesus. The man was very sad and disappointed. He did not want to obey.

Jesus then warned his friends of the danger of people thinking too much about their money and riches. This can keep them from trusting in God.

Jesus said it was very difficult for a rich man to enter the kingdom of heaven. The disciples were alarmed.

Find the question hidden round the question mark.

WHO THEN CAN BE SAVED?

___ ___

___ __

____

The computer
can't work out
the coded message - can you?
Solve the puzzle and find out what
Jesus said to his disciples.

2.8.5.16. 31 27.11.26. 31 5.16.8.12 31 8. 12. 31
_ _ _ _   _ _ _   _ _ _ _   _ _

8.27.10,9,12.12.8.25.19.3. 31 25.7.5. 31 26.9.5.
_ _ _ _ _ _ _ _ _ _   _ _ _   _ _ _

31 2.8.5.16. 31 15.9.13.20. 11.19.19. 31
_ _ _ _   _ _ _ _   _ _ _

5.16.8.26.15.12. 31 11.4.3. 31
_ _ _ _ _ _   _ _ _

10.9.12.12.8.25.19.3 31 2.8.5.16 31 15.9.13.
_ _ _ _ _ _ _ _   _ _ _ _   _ _ _

Why not write you own coded prayer?

Blind Bartimaeus (10.46-52)

Bartimaeus was a poor man. He was blind and could not work for a living. Every day he would sit by the roadside begging for money. One day Bartimaeus heard the news that Jesus was passing along the road near to him. He had heard that Jesus healed sick people, preached to the poor and helped those like himself. He hoped that he would meet Jesus. When Bartimaeus heard Jesus approaching, he shouted out to him. Some people told him to be quiet, but that made him shout all the more.

What did he shout to Jesus? Follow the direction of the arrows.

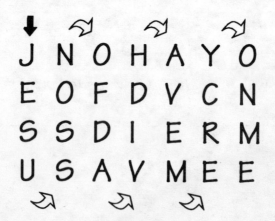

J N O H A Y O
E O F D V C N
S S D I E R M
U S A V M E E

_____ ___ __ _____

____ _____ __ __.

Jesus heard Bartimaeus and stopped in the road. 'What do you want me to do for you?' he asked. Bartimaeus told Jesus his greatest desire. 'I want to see.' That day, the blind man's prayer was answered.

What did Jesus say to him?
Put the blocks in the correct space.

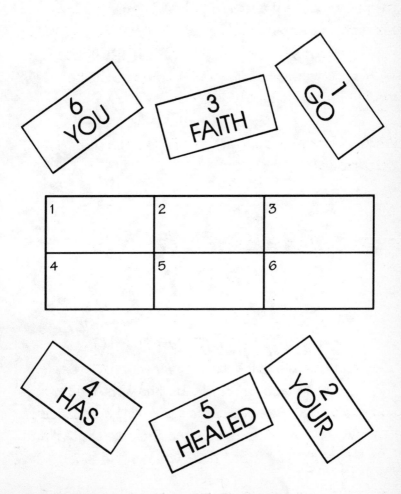

These words had an amazing effect on Bartimaeus.

What happened immediately?

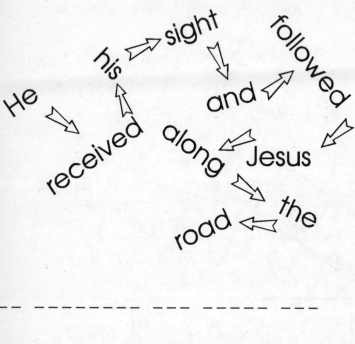

__ _____ ___ _____ ___

_____ _____ _____ ___

____

Triumphal Entry (11.1-11)

Jesus and his disciples made their way to Jerusalem. This was the place where Jesus knew that he would suffer and die. As they came near to the city, Jesus sent two of the disciples on ahead. 'Go to that village over there. At the first house you will find a colt tied up. No-one has ever ridden it.'

'If anyone questions you tell them...'

Unscramble the puzzle to find out.

11
6   r y l s o h t
i l w l
                8
      10   t i   **5**
      r e h e   n d a

   4   **3**
   t i   d e n e s

      2   **9**
   o r L d   c k a b

   7   **1**
   n d s e   h T e

_____

_____

The owners allowed the colt to go.

55

Coats were thrown over the colt's back and Jesus sat on it. Some people spread their coats on the road, and others laid down leafy branches that they had picked from the fields.

Some people led the way and others followed on behind shouting praise to God. They realised the importance of Jesus, who was the Son of God. 'HOSANNA' they shouted which means "Save us."

*Use the code to find out
what else they shouted*

H	O	S	A	N	N	A
1	2	3	4	5	5	A

Ble33ed   i3   1e   w12   c2me3

_ _ _ _ _ _ _   _ _   _ _   _ _ _   _ _ _ _ _

i5   t1e   54me   2f   t1e   L2rd.

_ _   _ _ _   _ _ _ _   _ _   _ _ _   _ _ _ _ .

Jesus rode into Jerusalem and went to the Temple.

Jesus Clears the Temple (11.15-19)

When Jesus reached the Temple he became very angry. The people had made it into a market place instead of being there to worship God. Some were buying and selling animals and birds to be used for sacrifices. Money changers had set up their stalls and were working busily. Jesus stormed through the Temple. He overturned the tables and benches.

H	D	O	E	U	N	S	O
■							E
R	God's house he said should be a _____. Start at H and use every second letter.						F
S							O
E	They had made it a _____. Start at D and take every second letter.						R
R							F
Y	E	A	B	R	B	P	O

The chief priest and teachers were afraid of Jesus. They hated him and wanted to find a way to kill him.

57

Parable of the Tenants (12.1-12)

Jesus told a story which pictured the situation of the time.

A man had a <u>vineyard</u> which he cared for very much. He rented the vineyard to some tenants while he went on a long <u>journey</u>. At harvest time he sent a <u>servant</u> to collect some of the <u>fruit</u> which was due to him as the owner. The tenants seized the man and sent him away empty-handed. They beat up the next one, then <u>killed</u> another. Each time the servant was treated very badly.

At last the <u>owner</u> decided to send his <u>son</u>. They will surely <u>respect</u> him, he thought.

But no. The tenants said to one another, 'Here comes the <u>heir</u>. If we kill him the vineyard will be ours.' So they carried out their wicked plot, and the owner's son was murdered.

God created and owns the world which he cares for very much. The church leaders were <u>tenants</u> in this world of God's. They owed him everything. The servants of God were badly treated by them - <u>people</u> did not listen to their <u>message</u>; some were killed, some were beaten. God sent his son to the world. Would they listen to him? No, he would be killed too.

The priest and leaders were even more determined to arrest Jesus and get rid of him.

Find the underlined words in the puzzle and score them out.

V	T	H	R	E	S	P	E	C	T	E
T	I	E	Y	W	E	S	R	E	T	A
N	F	N	L	R	A	O	I	D	E	O
A	F	T	E	P	H	N	E	H	N	C
V	R	O	W	Y	O	D	S	E	A	D
R	O	T	H	E	A	E	Y	I	N	E
E	R	E	N	W	O	R	P	R	T	L
S	L	E	F	T	H	I	D	M	S	L
J	O	U	R	N	E	Y	A	N	D	I
W	E	E	G	A	S	S	E	M	N	K
T	A	W	A	T	I	U	R	F	Y	#

Note down the letters left to find out what the church leaders did after Jesus told this story.

____ ____ _____ __ ___

_____ __ ____ ____ ___ ___

____ ____.

Paying Taxes to Caesar (12.13-17)

Some of the Pharisees and Jews hated Jesus and wanted to catch him out. They began by flattering him and then asked the question 'Should we pay taxes to Caesar (the Roman ruler) or not?' The tax was very unpopular with the Jews. Some of them believed that if they paid, it would be admitting that the Romans had a right to rule their land. Jesus knew that these men were just trying to trap him.

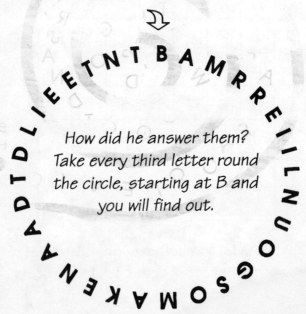

How did he answer them?
Take every third letter round
the circle, starting at B and
you will find out.

A denarius was a small coin something like our penny. They brought the coin to Jesus. 'Whose picture is this and whose inscription?' asked Jesus. 'Caesar's' they replied.

What then was Jesus' wise advice.

Unscramble the message

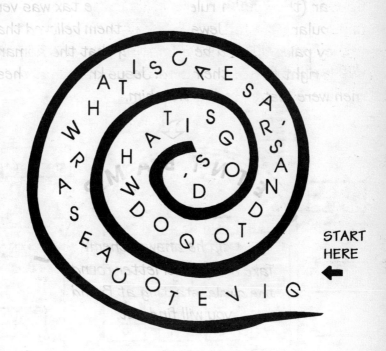

START
HERE

____ __ _____ ___ __

_____ ___ __ ___ ___ __

___.

They were amazed at this answer. They did not catch him out.

The Greatest
Commandment (12.28-34)

One teacher of the law asked Jesus, 'Which is the greatest commandment?'

Put the words in the correct order in the tablet to find Jesus' answer.

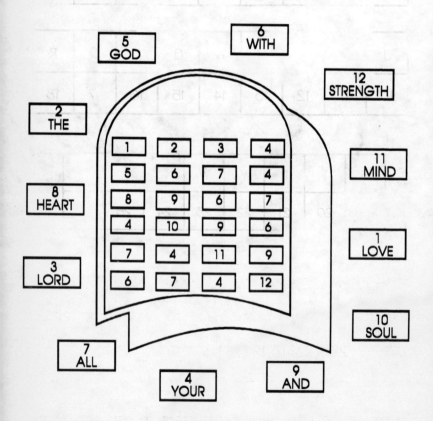

That is the most important thing for us to do.

Jesus also told the second most important commandment.

Work out the code.

A	B	C	D	E	F	G	H	I
1	2	3	4	5	6	7	8	9

J	K	L	M	N	O	P	Q	R
10	11	12	13	14	15	16	17	18

S	T	U	V	W	X	Y	Z
19	20	21	22	23	24	25	26

12.15.22.5.   25.15.21.18.   14.5.9.7.8.2.15.21.18

_ _ _ _   _ _ _ _   _ _ _ _ _ _ _ _ _

1.19.   25.15.21.18.19.5.12.6.

_ _   _ _ _ _ _ _ _ _

There is no commandment more important than these.

63

Widow's Offering (12.41-44)

Jesus sat watching as the people went into the temple and put their offerings of money into the collection box. Many rich people threw in large amounts, no doubt hoping that others would see how generous they were. One poor widow put in her offering.

Unscramble the letters to find what it was.

WOT RYVE LAMSL PREPCO INOCS

_____

They were not worth very much.
What did Jesus say about her offering?

R	W	I	D	O	W	H
O	R	E	A	S	U	A
O	T	E	O	T	R	S
P	E	H	█	H	Y	P
S	H	T	█	E	T	U
I	T	L	S	R	H	T
H	O	L	A	N	A	M
T	T	N	I	E	R	O

_____

_____

_____

_____

_____

Why did he say that? The other people had put in large sums of money.

Put the columns in the correct order.

1	2	3	4	5	6	7	8	9	10	11
S	H	E		P	U	T		I	N	
E	V	E	R	Y	T	H	I	N	G	
A	L	L		S	H	E	H	A	D	D
T	O		L	I	V	E		O	N	

6	3	10	8	11	2	5	4	9	1	7
U	E	N			H	P		I	S	T
T	E	G	I		V	Y	R	N	E	H
H	L	A		D	L	S		H	A	E
V		N			O	I	L	O	T	E

Her giving really cost her something.

Signs of the End of the Age (13.1-31)

Jesus privately instructed his friends Peter, James, John and Andrew about what would be the warning signs of the end of the world.

Can you crack the code?

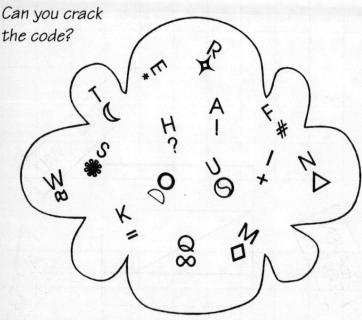

What signs did Jesus tell them to look for?

1) ⌀ ! ✗ ✸

2) ✗ ☺ ◻ ◺ ☺ ✗ ✸   ◺ #   ⌀ ! ✗ ✸

3) * ! ✗ ☾ ? ∞ ☺ ! = * ✸

4) # ! ◻ + ▷ * ✸

Jesus emphasised how important it was for the gospel to be preached to all nations of the world. The Son of Man (Jesus Christ) will come again with great power and glory.

Find another message when you complete the jigsaw.

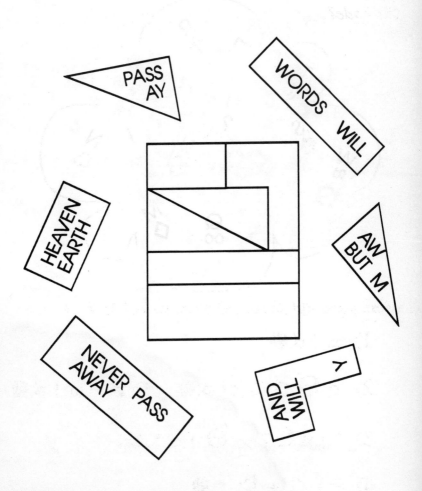

Day and Hour Unknown (13.32-37)

'No-one knows when the end times will be', Jesus tells us, 'except one Person.'

Who is that Person?
Follow the line for the answer.

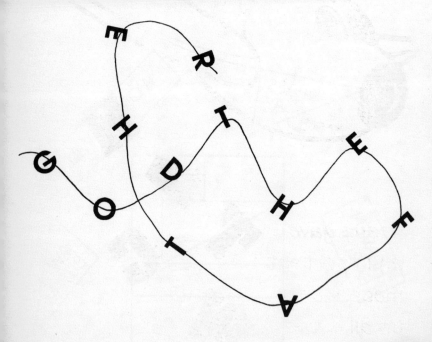

– – –   – – –   – – – – – –

We all have to be on guard - ready at any time.

Jesus gave
an important
message to
us all.

Look at the letters dropped
from the plane, and work out
what he said.

Jesus Anointed at Bethany (14.1-9)

Jesus went for a meal to the house of a man called Simon. A woman came up to him with a very expensive alabaster jar of perfumed ointment. This was a very precious possession. She broke the jar open and poured the perfume on Jesus' head. She did this to show how much she loved him. Some people spoke harshly to her - they thought it was a waste. But Jesus was pleased.

Sort out the words into the right order.

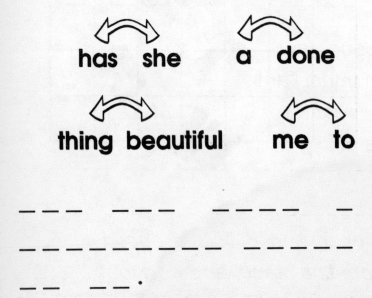

has she   a done

thing beautiful   me to

_ _ _ _ _ _ _ _ _ _ _

_ _ _ _ _ _ _ _ _ _ _ _ _ _

_ _ _ _ .

'You will be able to help the poor any time, but I will not always be with you,' Jesus added.

Work round the grid into the centre to find what else Jesus said.

E	D	P	E	R	F	U
R	A	N	D	T	O	M
U	H	Y	B	U	P	E
O	E	M		R	R	O
P	R	R		I	E	N
E	O	O	L	A	P	M
H	F	F	E	R	A	Y
S	E	B	Y	D	O	B

SHE POURED PERFUME ON MY BODY

BEFOREHAND TO PREPARE FOR MY

BURIAL.

Whenever the gospel is preached in the world, this story will be told in memory of this loving lady.

The Lord's Supper (14.12-26)

Jesus and his disciples went to a large upper room in a house in Jerusalem to eat the Passover feast together. Jewish families had this special feast every year to celebrate the time when the children of Israel were brought out of slavery in Egypt.

While they were having the meal what did Jesus do?

Take every third letter round the circle starting at T

_ _ _ _ _ _ _ _ _ _ _ _,

_ _ _ _ _ _ _ _ _,

_ _ _ _ _ _ _ _ _ _

_ _ _ _ _ _ _ _ _

_ _ _ _ _ _ _ _ _

What did Jesus say? Solve the code.

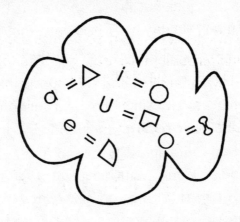

a = ▷   i = ◯
e = △   U = ▱   ◯ = 8

T▷k△ △▷t th◯s ◯'s
my b8dy

He then took the cup of wine, gave thanks for it and all the disciples drank from it.

What did Jesus say then? Use the same code.

Th◯s ◯s th△ bl88d
8f th△ c8v△n▷nt
wh◯ch ◯s p8▱r△d
8▱t f8r m▷ny

This is sometimes called the Last Supper which Jesus ate with his disciples but it is also the First Supper - the first of many times when Christians met together to eat the Lord's supper. They still do this today - remembering the Lord's death.

Gethsemane (14.32-42)

Jesus and his disciples went to the garden of Gethsemane. Jesus went to pray and asked his disciples to stay a little way off and keep watch. Jesus knew that he was soon to suffer greatly and was filled with dread. He prayed that God his Father would take this suffering away from him, but was still willing to be obedient.

What did he say?

```
↓     ↷      ↷      ↷      ↷      ↷
E  G  I  E  F  N  O  L  L  O  U
V  N  S  L  O  T  T  I  B  Y  W
E  I  P  B  R  E  W  W  U  T  I
R  H  O  I  Y  Y  H  I  T  A  L
Y  T  S  S  O  U  A  T  W  H  L
   ↷      ↷      ↷      ↷      ↷
```

When Jesus returned to the disciples he found them fast asleep.

What was Jesus' warning to his disciples?

Follow the arrows to find out.

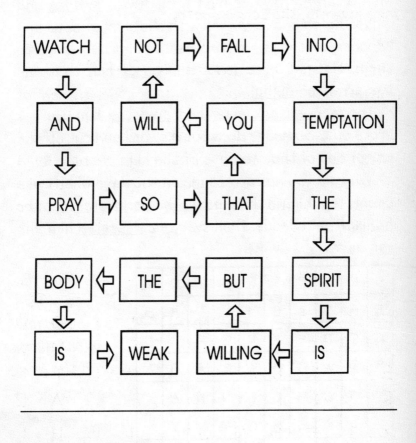

```
WATCH        NOT  ⇨  FALL  ⇨  INTO
  ⇩           ⇧               ⇩
AND          WILL ⇦  YOU     TEMPTATION
  ⇩           ⇧               ⇩
PRAY  ⇨  SO  ⇨  THAT          THE
                              ⇩
BODY ⇦  THE ⇦  BUT           SPIRIT
  ⇩           ⇧               ⇩
IS  ⇨  WEAK   WILLING ⇦  IS
```

_____

_____

_____

How Jesus suffered here, with no human companion able to comfort him.

Jesus arrested (14.43-52)

Judas Iscariot, one of the twelve disciples arrived then with a large crowd of men armed with swords and clubs. Judas had arranged with the chief priests and teachers of the law and elders to point out Jesus to them. He went up to Jesus and kissed him: that was the arranged signal.

The men seized Jesus and arrested him. Uproar broke out. Someone drew out a sword and cut off the ear of one of the servants of the high priest.

'Why did you not arrest me on the days when I was openly teaching in the temple. The Scriptures must be fulfilled' said Jesus. Then everyone deserted him and ran away.

S	E	L	P	I	C	S	I	D	I
E	H	D	L	E	J	U	D	A	S
R	S	D	E	A	R	E	R	L	C
U	W	W	C	S	W	R	A	O	A
T	O	O	M	E	E	N	N	A	R
P	R	R	S	S	G	R	M	Y	I
I	D	C	T	I	B	E	T	T	O
R	S	E	S	T	U	C	R	E	T
C	D	A	K	I	S	S	E	D	D
S	Y	D	E	Z	I	E	S	E	R

Find the words underlined in the story in the grid. Write down the letters remaining in the grid to find out what Jesus said when he saw Judas coming.

_____

At the Court (14.53-65)

Jesus was taken to the court of the high priest where all the important men came to hear what he would say. All the lawyers and teachers were wanting to find an excuse to put Jesus to death. They could find nothing. Many people told lies against him but their stories did not agree. The high priest asked Jesus to answer the accusations made against him.

What did Jesus do? Read the sentence backwards starting at the end.

REWSNA   ON   EVAG   DNA
TNELIS   DENIAMER   SUSEJ

He did not need to make excuses. Again the high priest asked a question.

	1	2	3	4	5	6	7	8	9	10	11
a	A	r			y		u				
b	C		r	i	s						
c	s		n			f		G		d	?

Fill in the missing letters.

e at 3a, 11a, 10b,
h at 10a, 2b, 9b.
o at 6a, 2c, 5c, 9c.
t at 9a, 6b, 8b.

77

Jesus answered I AM. He was immediately accused of blasphemy - saying he was equal with God. They all condemned him to death.

Peter Denies Jesus (14.66-72)

Peter was in the courtyard warming himself by the fire while Jesus was inside being questioned by the high priest. A servant girl came up to him and looked at him closely.

Y	W	A	O	I	R	U	T	E
Z								A
E		*Starting at the top left hand corner,*						H
S		*note down every third letter to find out*						N
A		*what the girl said to Peter.*						L
R		_____						T
U		_____						E
N								S
E	S	T	W	E	A	O	J	H

I	H	L	D	A	K	O	T
A							T
W							I
T	*Do the same in this square*						N
T	*to find Peter's reply.*						Y
T							N
W	_____						O
U							O
E	_____						G
O							T
O	_____						T
O	R	N	B	A	K	A	U

The girl tackled him once more. Again Peter denied knowing Jesus. Then some others standing around accused Peter of being a follower of Jesus, but he denied it with curses.

What happened then?
Beginning in the centre,
read round
the spiral.

___ _____

_____ ___

_____

____.

This immediately brought to Peter's mind something that Jesus had said to him days before.

H	E	C	O	C	K
T	L	D	I	S	C
E	L	T	I	O	R
R	I	E	M	W	O
O	W	E	E	N	W
F	U	R	S	M	S
E	O	H	T	E	T
B	Y	E	C	I	W

↑

Work round the grid into the centre

_ _ _ _ _ _   _ _ _

_ _ _ _   _ _ _ _ _

_ _ _ _ _   _ _ _

_ _ _ _

_ _ _ _ _ _

_ _   _ _ _ _ _

_ _ _ _ _

When he realised what he had done, he broke down and wept.

Jesus Before Pilate (15.1-20)

Jesus was led away to appear before Pilate, the Roman governor of the region. He was cruelly treated.

Match up the boxes to find out more.

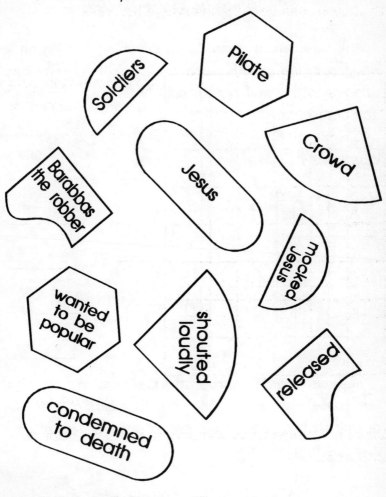

Soldiers

Pilate

Crowd

Barabbas the robber

Jesus

mocked Jesus

wanted to be popular

shouted loudly

released

condemned to death

Jesus - _____

Barabbas - _____

Pilate - _____

Crowd - _____

Soldiers - _____

Crucifixion (15.21-32)

Jesus was taken away to be crucified - hung on a wooden cross until he died. Simon from Cyrene was passing into town from the country. He was forced to do something.

What was it?

A	C	E
J	O	R
S	U	Y

_ _ _ _ _

_ _ _ _ _

_ _ _ _ _

Jesus was nailed to a cross at a place called Golgotha. Two robbers were crucified on either side of him. The notice written above his cross showed the charge against him.

Hold this up to a mirror to read what it said.

THE KING

OF THE JEWS

The priests and the teachers did not understand that Jesus was indeed the Son of God, the Messiah chosen by God to save his people from their sin. They mocked him.

Unscramble the letters to find one of the cruel things that they said about Jesus.

E H   V A D E S   E T O H S R   U T B

_ _   _ _ _ _ _   _ _ _ _ _ _   _ _ _

E H   N A T C   V E S A   S H E L F I M

_ _   _ _ _ _   _ _ _ _   _ _ _ _ _ _ _

Death of Jesus (15.33-41)

At twelve noon on the day Jesus died darkness came over the whole land for three hours. At 3 o'clock in the afternoon Jesus cried out in a loud voice in the depths of his sufferings.

Fit the columns in the correct places.

1	2	3	4	5	6	7	8	9	10	11	12	13

7	4	12	6	13	2	9	11	3	8	1	10	5
	G	O	D	D	Y	Y	G		M	M		O
V	U	A		H		O	Y	E	W	Y		H
E	S	?	K		O		E	R	N	F	M	A

Then with a loud cry, Jesus died. The temple curtain was torn in two from top to bottom.

The Roman soldier who witnessed Jesus' death was very affected by what he saw and heard.

Arrange the words properly to find out what he said.

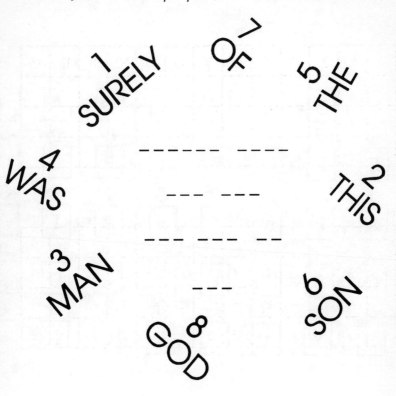

1 SURELY
7 OF
5 THE
4 WAS
2 THIS
3 MAN
6 SON
8 GOD

‗‗‗‗‗‗ ‗‗‗‗

‗‗‗ ‗‗‗

‗‗‗ ‗‗‗ ‗‗

‗‗‗

Burial of Jesus (15.42-47)

Joseph from Arimathea was an important official.
Towards evening on the day that Jesus died, he did
something very brave.

What was that?

Follow the arrows.

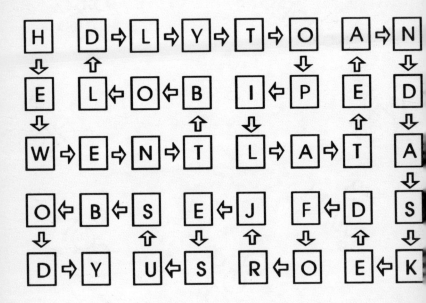

_____

_____

Pilate was surprised to hear that Jesus was dead already. After he had checked with the soldiers, he gave the body to Joseph. Joseph lovingly took Jesus' body from the cross, wrapped it in linen and placed it in a tomb cut out of the rock.

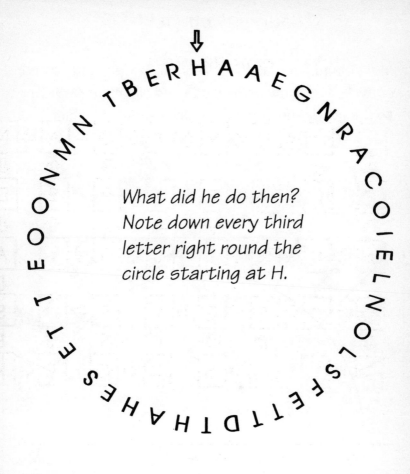

What did he do then? Note down every third letter right round the circle starting at H.

_____

_____

Mary Magdalene and another Mary who was also a follower of Jesus, watched him.

Resurrection (16.1-20)

Mary Magdalene, another lady called Mary and Salome came to the tomb with spices and ointments wanting to anoint Jesus' body to show their love to him.

When did they come?

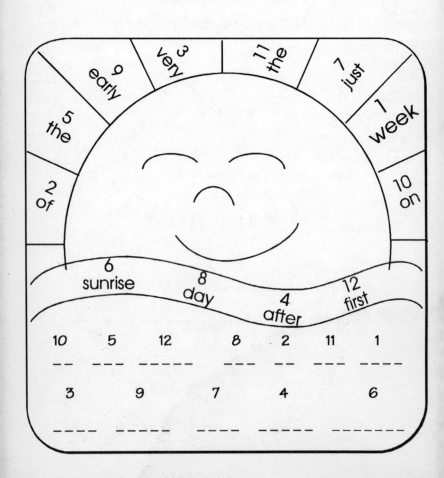

They were worried about the big stone at the entrance to the tomb but when they got there, what did they find? The letters of the words have been wrongly separated.

Can you put them in the correct order?

Thes   ton   eha   dbe   enro   lleda   way.

_____

Inside the tomb sat an angel dressed in a white robe. The women were scared.

Follow the trail to find the message the angel gave to the women.

START HERE ⬆

Jesus had indeed risen from the dead. Many people saw him in the following days. Jesus' message to his disciples then and to Christians now is :-

Start at G and note every 3rd letter round the world.

-- ---- --- --- ----- ---
----- --- --- ---- -- ---
---------.

After Jesus spoke he was taken up to heaven.

ANSWERS

ANSWERS

Page

7.   Good news, gospel

8.   Coat of camels hair, leather belt, locusts, wild honey

9.   After me will come one more powerful than I, the thong of whose sandals I am not worthy to stoop down and untie.

10.   You are my son whom I love with you I am well pleased.

11.   Repent and believe the good news.

12.   Come follow me and I will make you fishers of men.

13.   At once they left their nets and followed Jesus.

14.   Son your sins are forgiven.

15.   Get up. Take your mat and go home.

17.   Jesus said, 'Go into all the world and preach the good news to all creation.'Then the disciples went out. Repent

18.   Path - birds ate it.

Rocky place - scorched, withered

Thorny ground - choked.

Good ground - good crop.

19.   Satan / Trouble and persecution / Worries of this life deceitfulness of wealth, desires for other things.

20.   Love, joy, peace, patience, kindness.

22.   The word of God is living and active, it judges the thoughts and attitudes of the heart.

23.   The kingdom of the world has become the kingdom of

our Lord and of his Christ and he will reign for ever and ever.

24. Scared. Asleep.

25. Faith. Power

26. What do you want with me Jesus son the most high God?

27. Sitting dressed in his right mind.

28. Go home to your family and tell them how much the Lord has done for you and how he has had mercy on you.

29. My little daughter is dying.
    Don't be afraid, just believe.

30. Mother, Father, Peter, James, John.
    Little girl get up.
    Give her something to eat.

31. If I just touch his clothes I will be healed.

32. Who touched my clothes.

33. Daughter your faith has healed you. Go in peace.

34. He said, 'Come with me by yourselves to a quiet place and get some rest.'

35. 5 loaves. 2 fishes.

36. Gave thanks. 12 baskets

37. Take courage it is I. Don't be afraid.

38. Yes Lord but even the dogs under the table eat the children's crumbs.

40. Jesus gave thanks, broke the bread, gave it to his disciples to give to the crowd.

41. Seven basketfuls of broken pieces of food left over.

42. John the Baptist. Elijah. Prophet. You are the Christ.

43. This is my son whom I love. Listen to him.

44. If anyone wants to be first, he must be the very last and the servant of all.

45. If you welcome a little child in my name you welcome me and God who sent me.

46. Let the little children come to me and do not hinder them for the kingdom of God belongs to such as these.

47. A little child.
Jesus took the children in his arms put his hands on them and blessed them.

48. What must I do to inherit eternal life?

49 Who then can be saved?

51. With man this is impossible but not with God. All things are possible with God.

52. Jesus son of David have mercy on me.

53. Go, your faith has healed you.

54 He received his sight and followed Jesus along the road.

55. The Lord needs it, and will send it back here shortly.

56. Blessed is he who comes in the name of the Lord.

57. House of prayer. Den of robbers.

59. They were afraid of the crowd so they left him and went away.

60. Bring me a denarius and let me look at it.

61 Give to Caesar what is Caesar's and to God what is God's.

62. Love the Lord your God with all your heart and with all your soul and with all your mind and with all your strength.

63. Love your neighbour as yourself.

64. Two very small copper coins.
This poor widow has put more into the treasury than all the others.

65. She put in everything. All had to live on.

66. Wars. Rumours of wars. Earthquakes. Famines

67. Heaven and earth will pass away but my words will never pass away.

68 God the Father.

69. Watch.

70. She has done a beautiful thing to me.

71. She poured perfume on my body beforehand to prepare for my burial.

72. Took the bread, gave thanks, broke it and gave it to the disciples.

73. Take eat, this is my body.
This is the blood of the covenant which is poured out for many.

74. Everything is possible for you, yet not what I will but what you will.

75. Watch and pray so that you will not fall into temptation. The spirit is willing but the body is weak.

76. Here comes my betrayer.

77. Jesus remained silent and gave no answer.
Are you the Christ the son of God?

78. You also were with that Nazarene, Jesus.
79. I do not know what you are talking about.
    The cock crowed the second time.
80. Before the cock crows twice you will disown me three times.
81. Jesus - condemned to death.
    Barnabas - released
    Pilate - wanted to be popular
    Crowd - shouted loudly
    Soldiers - mocked Jesus.
82. Carry Jesus' cross.
    The King of the Jews.
83. He saved others but he can't save himself.
84. My God, my God, why have you forsaken me?
85. Surely this man was the son of God.
86. He went boldly to Pilate and asked for Jesus' body.
87. He rolled a stone against the entrance of the tomb.
88. On the first day of the week, very early, just after sunrise.
89. The stone had been rolled away.
    Do not be alarmed, you are looking for Jesus who was crucified. He has risen. He is not here. See the place where they laid him. Go tell his disciples and Peter he is going to Galilee. There you will see him.
90. Go into all the world and preach the good news to all creation.